Great & Capital Changes:

An Account of the Valley Forge Encampment

Barbara Pollarine

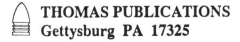

THOMAS PUBLICATIONS
Gettysburg PA 17325

Contents

Introduction

"...Unless some great and capital change suddenly takes place in that line, this Army must inevitably be reduced to one or other of these three things. Starve, dissolve or disperse..."

So General Washington described the state of the Continental Army to the President of Congress, Henry Laurens, on December 23, 1777. The Army had arrived at Valley Forge only days before on December 19, after a long, arduous campaign. Problems with supplying the troops had been evident since early in the fall and they worsened as winter approached. Feeding the men was only one of the problems facing the Commander-in-Chief as the encampment began. Difficulties with Congress, threats to his leadership, discontented officers, a crumbling support system and the need to better prepare the troops to meet the enemy in the coming campaign also beset Washington as he penned his dire letter to Congress.

Triumph over adversity is the stuff legends are made of. The situation at the outset of the Valley Forge winter, however, is not the complete, nor most significant, part of the story of the famed Revolutionary War encampment. Problems of varying kinds plagued the army throughout the eight years of the struggle for independence. What sets the winter of 1777-78 apart are the strides that were made toward placing the army on a footing from which eventual success could be won.

The encampment afforded an opportunity for Washington and his staff to meet and overcome serious problems as well as move the army along the necessary path toward an organization which could win the war. Time, adequate forces, the availability of individuals with needed skills, the realization of the requirements of the supply network and logistics necessary to keep the army in the field, and Congressional cooperation combined to make changes that would not only keep the army from dissolving, but assure its progression from a seasonal, militia-type organization into a professional fighting force.

The Stage Is Set

By the fall of 1776, it was clear that the new nation needed to adapt its war plans and forces to the realities of a long term struggle with Great Britain. The defeats in New York at both Long Island and White Plains spurred Washington and Congress into cooperating on a number of reform measures for the Continental Army. These defeats showed the need for a large body of trained, disciplined Continentals. As John Adams put it, the country needed "...a regular Army, and the most masterly Discipline, because...without these We cannot reasonably hope to be a powerful, a prosperous, or a free People."

Congress enacted legislation reforming the army in October 1776. One of the most important changes made was to recruit for the duration of the war rather than maintain single year enlistments. This marked a fundamental difference in attitude toward the military. Previously, Americans had insisted on the ideal of a citizen soldiery called upon as needed and sent home at the end of the campaign. The fear of a "standing army" in the new republic was quite strong. However, practical experience had shown the need for a more permanent force. Changes in the Articles of War to improve discipline, regimental reorganizations, increased officers' salaries, and annual uniform allowances were also included in the plans for reforming the army.

At the end of the year, Washington's timely victories over the British at Trenton and Princeton forced the enemy to retire into winter quarters at New Brunswick, New Jersey. The Continentals settled into quarters at Morristown, New Jersey. Washington began implementing reforms and rebuilding his forces for the coming campaign.

Meanwhile, the British War Office was planning a campaign to split the colonies by using a three pronged offensive led by its generals, Burgoyne, St. Leger, and Howe. They were to move on Albany, New York from both the north and the south. Sir William Howe chose not to follow the plan, but rather to pursue an independent course. American forces already positioned in the northern New York area would eventually have to meet and deal with Burgoyne and St. Leger, while Washington and the main army watched and waited for Howe to make his objective clear.

George Washington

George Washington (1732-1799) assumed the position of Commander-in-Chief of the Continental Army in June 1775. From his first encounter with American troops, he spoke of establishing discipline and professionalism in the forces. Based on his French and Indian War experiences, he knew that only unyielding commitment to hard work and attention to administrative detail kept troops in the field. Armed with this knowledge and exemplary leadership ability, Washington managed to not only keep the army in the field, but bring them from a seasonal, militia-based force to a professional military organization.

George Washington. Painting by James Peale (c. 1787).

Campaign for Philadelphia: The Road to Valley Forge

After weeks of waiting, Washington received notice that Howe and his troops had finally left New York City. Uncertain of their objective, Washington concluded that they were headed south, toward the capital city of Philadelphia. He began moving his troops in the direction of the city. In early August, intelligence reports came in stating that the British fleet had been sighted near the entrance to Chesapeake Bay, however, they turned back out to sea. The Americans continued their watchful waiting.

By late August, the British fleet arrived in the Chesapeake Bay with their troops disembarking at Head of Elk (Elkton), Maryland on August 28, 1777. Knowing of British movement in the bay, Washington moved his troops south, passing through Philadelphia, to meet Howe's army. At that point, the campaign of 1777 began in earnest.

Howe, following a deliberate course, did not move until early September, when he headed north into southeastern Pennsyl-

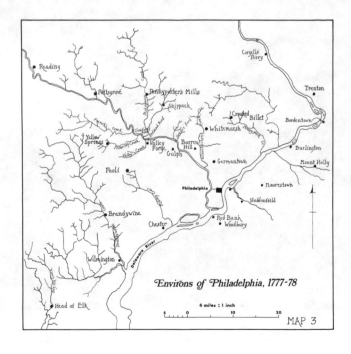

Environs of Philadelphia, 1777-78

6 miles : 1 inch

MAP 3

6

vania. By September 10th, both armies were in the area of the Brandywine Creek, with the Americans managing to keep between the British and Philadelphia. An engagement appeared to be drawing near. Howe needed to turn east toward his objective of Philadelphia; Washington and the Americans suspected such a move and began making preparations based on that assumption.

Washington's plans for deploying his troops for the coming engagement were based on the information that the Brandywine Creek was crossable only at a fixed series of fords. He, therefore, concentrated his forces near those points. Howe, having the benefit of more accurate intelligence, located untended fords further north. The British plan intended that Howe march toward the untended fords, cross the creek and surprise the Americans. To assure a surprise, Howe left part of the army under the command of Wilhelm Von Knyphausen to fake an attack and draw Washington's attention.

The Americans took the bait and engaged Knyphausen's troops. In the meantime, Howe continued his march northward, unnoticed, despite the fact that some intelligence had reached American headquarters and reported that the British were marching in that direction. By mid-afternoon, Howe was in position and began attacking the startled American right flank.

As the Americans struggled to turn and meet the assault, Howe's troops took up valuable time to form into columns intended to smash the exposed flank. They had a bit of trouble because the men were already exhausted from the 12-14 mile march that they completed before reaching their position. The delay benefited American commanders because it gave them time to reorganize and rush reinforcements to the point of battle. Consequently, instead of a rout, the Continentals devised and executed a hasty, though hotly contested, retreat.

The retreat began to fall apart due to inadequate communication between the Americans. Regiments and battalions had to be grouped and positioned as best they could, improvising as necessary. As a result, the Americans conducted their fall-back with some degree of order, managing to maintain a defensive line joined by Washington and his reinforcements. The quick thinking of some American officers and the courage of large numbers of their men allowed the Continentals to conduct a professional retreat toward the village of Dilworth.

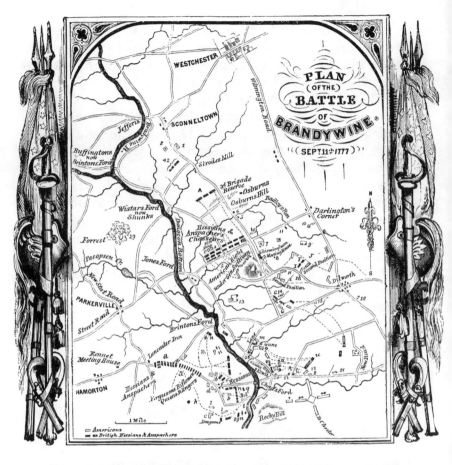

Plan of the Battle of Brandywine, Sept. 11, 1777: Washington took the bait of Knyphausen's feint and engaged at Chadds Ford. In the meantime, Howe and Cornwallis marched north with the other portion of the army and crossed the Brandywine at Trimble's and Jeffrie's Fords. By mid-afternoon Howe was in position to assault the exposed American right flank. Washington rushed reinforcements to meet the attack, but was never able to conduct much more than a stubborn resistance and a professional retreat. At nightfall the battlefield was in the hands of the British.

The Battle of the Brandywine ended with the British maintaining the field, however, the Americans had inflicted some damage to the enemy and managed to withdraw relatively intact toward Chester. Howe, primarily because of the exhaustion of his troops, had not dealt the Continentals a crushing blow. The British army camped on the battlefield and collected itself over the next few days while the Americans regrouped at Chester and moved back toward Philadelphia.

Although Washington reported to Congress on September 11th that he had been "obliged to leave the enemy masters of the field," reaction by both sides over the next several days indicated that the Americans had shown themselves well in difficult circumstances. Morale was high and the Continentals looked forward to the next opportunity to engage the enemy and make up for the loss.

Over the next two weeks, the armies continued their jockeying for position between the Chester valley and Philadelphia. Washington set about pressing Congress for more troops and garnering further reinforcements from Continentals stationed in the "north," i.e. New York. Meanwhile, the state of Pennsylvania's government hurriedly prepared to defend Philadelphia by calling out the local militia to guard the fords and ferries above the town. Washington also worried about the Delaware river forts and obstructions below the city. All prepared for the next act in the unfolding fight for the capital.

By September 16, both armies were in eastern Chester County close enough to one another to trigger the next engagement in the fray. British and American scouting parties met up and began to draw in other detachments for what appeared to be the expected battle. However, the skies opened up and a torrential rain began which lasted throughout the day and into the night. Both sides had their ammunition destroyed by the storm and the threatened battle was washed out. Hence, the action known as the "Battle of the Clouds" never actually occurred.

Both armies continued their tete-a-tete through Chester county. Washington, concerned about inland storehouses at Reading and other locations, sent a detachment on September 18, headed by Henry Lee and Alexander Hamilton, to the village of Valley Forge to remove valuable commodities, including flour, for the Continentals. The British, pushing toward the Schuylkill River, also sent a large detachment to remove military stores. The two parties met

Henry Lee (1756-1818). Painting by Charles Willson Peale (1783).

Anthony Wayne (1745-96). Painting attributed to James Sharples, Sr. (1795-96).

as the Americans were putting the supplies on barges. After a brief exchange, the Americans were driven off and the Redcoats helped themselves to the goods.

On September 19, Washington marched his troops north, and crossed the Schuylkill at Parker's Ford where he hoped to aid the militia in guarding the fords across which the enemy would have to move, closer to the city. The commander left a contingent of Pennsylvania troops under General Anthony Wayne south of the river to harass the British rear and monitor their movements. Again, with the aid of superior local intelligence, Howe learned of the location of Wayne's camp near Paoli. During the night, the enemy surprised the Americans, inflicted heavy casualties, and earned the raid the infamous title, "The Paoli Massacre."

Congress fled from Philadelphia on September 17, with the state government not far behind. With the political authorities gone, the importance of the capital diminished. Washington had to now weigh his options—further direct efforts toward defending the city or opt for protecting the interior with its valuable storehouses. The consideration of the possible threat to both and their relative importance effected the events of the next several days.

Once more, Howe decided to fake a movement toward another target in the hopes that Washington would take the bait. On the 21st, British detachments began to move upriver; Washington, worried about the stores at Reading and allowing the enemy to position itself between the Americans and interior Pennsylvania, chose to keep the army on the upper reaches of the Schuylkill. Howe, too, was concerned about supplying his troops and needed to reestablish contact with the fleet; he pushed on toward the city. Howe and his army crossed the river on September 22nd and Philadelphia's fate was sealed.

Washington continued to seek reinforcements while Howe slowly made his way to the city stopping for several days in Norriton Township to further assess the situation. By September 23rd, he had established a defensive line between the Americans and Philadelphia through Norristown. Howe left his main army at Germantown on the 25th and sent a detachment into the city the following day to officially assume control.

In the interim, Washington's long awaited reinforcements of both Continentals and militia arrived. This prompted him to call a Council of War on September 28th to discuss with his general officers whether to mount an immediate attack or await further reinforcements. The council advised against an attack and recommended that the army move to within twelve miles of the city to be ready for any opportunity that presented itself.

By the beginning of October, pressure was building on Washington to engage the enemy. Congress was upset with being ousted from the capital, the state government feared for its own, the "northern" army was making significant progress against Burgoyne, and the main army was lacking any tangible success. Washington determined to strike at the enemy at the first favorable moment.

Howe, on the other hand, having settled into the city was even more dependent on securing his water-borne supply line. During the campaign, the British secured supplies from the countryside, but now they needed to make certain access to the city from the Delaware River remained open. Complicating this problem, the Americans held the two river forts of Mifflin and Mercer.

On October 3rd, Howe made his move on the river forts creating an opportunity for Washington at Germantown. The American plan for the battle was complicated and required coordinated attacks on the enemy flanks to drive them back toward the city. It was felt that the British, once on the retreat, would be unable to meet an attack coming from several directions.

After dark on the 3rd, the Continentals began their march with the attack to commence at 5 A.M. on October 4th. The battle began in a dense early morning fog with gunsmoke soon making visibility even worse. General John Sullivan, leading the attack on the enemy center, had little difficulty in reaching his position on schedule, but the column under General Nathanael Greene, which was to move in from the north, lost its way and was delayed. However, by all contemporary accounts, the British were surprised and fell back under heavy fire.

The attack missed its mark when the two main columns, approaching along different roads, failed to join smoothly; one wing overlapped the other and fell in behind it. With visibility greatly reduced, confusion ensued. The American army hesitated and began to retreat.

As the Americans faltered, reinforcements reached the British. They counterattacked and turned the tide. Although the Continentals were again forced to retreat as at Brandywine, there was a clear difference. They attempted a highly complex maneuver, surprised the enemy, and came very close to defeating them. Rather than feeling down about the victory snatched from them, most American officers were heartened by the stand that they held against the British. Even Washington's own comments reflect a sense of achievement and optimism as written a week after the battle, "We must not repine [over the retreat], but on the contrary rejoice that we have given a severe blow to our enemies and that our Ranks are as full or rather fuller than they were before the engagement."

This spirit of optimism spread through the army and into reports to Congress regarding the action and some began to look forward to the next engagement. The army remained in a state of readiness and welcomed more reinforcements into the ranks over the next two weeks. In addition, news arrived on October 15th that General Horatio Gates had defeated Burgoyne at Saratoga which created another incentive to again engage the enemy and deal them a decisive blow. However, circumstances combined to negate any possibility for an attack. Howe chose to concentrate on fortifying his hold on Philadelphia and smashing the river forts to secure his

The British defense of the Chew House at the Battle of Germantown was an unnecessary stumbling-block for the Americans.

Horatio Gates (1728-1806). Painting by Charles Willson Peale (c. 1782).

supply line. He was also loathe to expose his forces to another drubbing as had taken place at Germantown. He, too, called for necessary reinforcements to bolster his troops, which, at this point, were also experiencing supply problems. Thus, time and British priorities conspired to rob the Americans of their much sought after opportunity to attack.

By the beginning of November, the Continentals established camp at Whitemarsh and the focus of the struggle shifted to the forts on the Delaware. Howe had to take those positions before winter set in and the river became frozen, making it impossible for the British fleet to provision his army. English land and naval forces mounted a withering assault on Fort Mifflin which fell on November 15. The garrison at Fort Mercer, on the New Jersey side, held until November 20, and with a secure water route, Howe and the British army held the city.

From Whitemarsh, Washington continued small unit operations intended to aggravate British supply problems. It was impossible for Howe to provision his troops and the civilian populace solely by river transport; he was dependent on continuing to secure supplies from the surrounding countryside. On the American side, the logistical crisis deepened with shortages of all materials, and thus, by harassing enemy efforts to gather supplies, they not only hurt British opportunities to obtain stores, but effectively dispersed their own forces and made them more easily provisioned.

Congress, not realizing the tenuous situation of the Continental Army, continued to press for a "winter's campaign." Washington had been polling his officers, through a circular letter dated October 26, 1777, about the possibilities for a winter's campaign as well as other matters. It was generally observed that a winter's campaign was impractical from a number of standpoints because there were too many problems that needed immediate attention: troops were worn out from the movements of the campaign, the supply system was crumbling, and it was necessary to contain the British while protecting the interior of the state.

A Congressional committee arrived at Whitemarsh on December 3rd charged with pressing for a winter campaign. Within a day, the British formed to attempt another foray against the Americans in order to test their strength and the possibility of striking a decisive blow. Both generals could have used a victory, but both also were not willing to take unreasonable risks. As a result, the committee observed a series of skirmishes between the two forces from December 5-8. These skirmishes illustrated the army's strengths and weaknesses and ultimately convinced all parties involved of the impossibility of the anticipated campaign.

Winter Cantonment

The question of where the army would winter was finally about to be answered. Clearly, the decision was complex and required a great deal of compromise to achieve a suitable solution. Washington had been querying his officers since late October on the matter. Both the Continental Congress and the state government had concerns about where and how the army would spend the next several weeks, as well as whether or not it would be able to remain intact, given its perilous supply situation. Not to mention the question of containing the British army in Philadelphia. All of these issues, and many others, had to be confronted and addressed before a decision could be made regarding the army's disposition for the winter.

Political considerations were of the utmost importance since the army depended on the civilian government and populace for its very existence. The state wanted and expected protection of the countryside surrounding Philadelphia; it felt that the army must remain as close as possible, within a relatively safe distance to the enemy, because the state was primarily responsible for the immediate support of the army. Congress believed much the same because of its residence within the state, as well as its firm resolve to press for a winter campaign. Washington sought their opinions before deciding upon a final compromising solution.

Military needs also had to be taken into account because strategically, the army had to be close enough to the enemy to contain them but far enough away that a surprise attack was an impossibility. Logistically, they needed to position themselves in such a way that they could take advantage of established storehouses in the interior of the state and whatever could be gleaned from the surrounding countryside. Since the decision was still pending on an encampment location, no system of ancillary magazines had been set up to help in provisioning the army. Finally, after a strenuous, mobile campaign, the army needed an area large enough to accommodate several thousand men without billeting them with civilians. As John Laurens, aide to Washington, put it to his father, Henry Laurens, President of Congress, in early December, the army required "...a position which will not absolutely expose us to a Winters Campaign, but furnish us excellent

Henry Laurens (1724-92). Painting by Charles Willson Peale (c. 1784). President of Congress, Laurens heeded Washington's pleas for assistance by dispatching a committee to camp to deal with the problems of the army.

Quarters for our men at the same time that it leaves us within distance for taking considerable advantages of the enemy-and covering a valuable and extensive Country."

In response to Washington's request for recommendations on where the army should winter, Pennsylvania General Anthony Wayne suggested an area 20 miles west of Philadelphia as a likely location. It was located in agriculturally rich Chester County, and it was hoped that supplies could be obtained from the countryside. The Valley Forge vicinity provided what was needed both politically and militarily. It was within a day's march of the enemy; close enough to keep the pressure on, but far enough to prevent a surprise attack. The terrain was rough and the Schuylkill River provided a border as well as a vital transport and communications line. The area was also large and open—a requirement that officers felt was important for a "proper cantonment" of their troops; shelter could be constructed which would spare them from the ravages of field conditions. Overall, Valley Forge satisfied the requirements of those involved in deciding the army's immediate fate. Washington achieved an important accomplishment through this compromise: he had balanced both military and political interests by forging a workable solution to the question of the army's winter quarters. As the winter wore on, this compromise would also bear further fruit.

On December 11, Washington set the army in motion toward its winter home, stopping temporarily at Gulph Mills while final arrangements were made for the establishment of the camp. On December 19, the army reached Valley Forge. The organization that arrived was indeed in dire straits, although it was not, by any means, a ragged or pathetic force. It had fought well and with spirit during the campaign of 1777, and the results were illustrated by the fact that General Howe was barricaded in Philadelphia after suffering considerably at Brandywine and Germantown. The challenge that faced them at this point was much less glorious, but none the less important: the business of securing their future for the next few months, and ultimately the next several years.

Great and Capital Changes

As the Continental Army settled into winter quarters, Washington began to take action on the tremendous challenges facing the American War machine. He fired his first volley, meant to spur Congress into motion, by writing his famous letter of December 22, 1777–dramatic testimony describing the trying circumstances confronting the troops was shot off to the President of Congress. Washington's words prompted Congress to appoint a Committee on Conference and send them to Valley Forge to deal with the crisis. According to the Commander-in-Chief, he invited Congress to come to camp to work out with him, "The most perfect plan that can be devised for correcting all abuses."

In preparation, Washington and his staff set about the task of "preparing and digesting matters" for the committee. They collected information and opinions on issues facing the army. The matters at hand included attacking deficiencies of the support system; i.e., supply problems, addressing the concerns and complaints of the officer corps; reorganizing regiments; and acting on the long planned retraining of the army.

Since early on in the war effort, supply and transport problems plagued the army. Critical support departments had to be created from the ground up. Congress established departments and made appointments as needed rather than following an organized plan. As a result, the system grew haphazardly and there was little room for error. Supplying and transporting the army evolved into an intricate, complex network that criss-crossed the colonies. This patchwork system was further undermined by the disruption in the economy brought on by the war and Congress' inability to recognize that they had a year round, rather than seasonal, fighting force to support.

By the time the army encamped at Valley Forge, the neglect of the support departments throughout the preceding year brought on a severe supply crisis. Congress left key jobs vacant and failed to see the need for reform. Washington described the impending crisis to Congress as early as October of 1777. He observed the effects of the crumbling system first hand, following the Battle of Germantown, which had cost the army three days of provisions. Washington dispersed his troops around the Philadelphia area in order to adequately provide for them. By spreading troops out, he

Military Aides

Throughout the war, Washington depended upon a series of military aides-de-camp, or secretaries, to carry out the business of the army. The aides, mostly young, talented volunteers, checked accounts, examined deserters and prisoners, carried and delivered orders, drafted and copied correspondence, translated letters, arranged for the location of Headquarters, and attended to a myriad of other administrative details.

The hard work and dedication required of an aide, combined with Washington's familiar affection for his "military family," created an *esprit de corps* that proved invaluable. Some aides, such as Tench Tilghman, remained with the commander for nearly the entire war; Washington inspired intense loyalty and commitment. At Valley Forge, nine aides lived and worked with the General, assisting with the administration of the army.

John Laurens (1754-82). Painting by Charles Willson Peale (c. 1784), replica.

Alexander Hamilton (1757-1804). Painting by Charles Willson Peale (c. 1778). Typical of Washington's aides, young and talented Hamilton volunteered to serve on the General's staff for most of the war.

Military staff used rooms in headquarters as needed for workrooms, meeting space, and dining.

Varnum's Quarters: Built early in the 18th century, this heavily restored farmhouse hosted General James Varnum and his aides early on in the camp.

could better supply them from surrounding communities, as well as interrupt the flow of goods into the city. This action only put off the inevitable. Shortly after the establishment of camp, the situation deteriorated. As General Jedediah Huntington of Connecticut described it, "we live from hand to mouth, and are like to do so, for all anything I see." Thorough reform of the supply departments was fundamentally necessary; without improvement in this vital area, the army could not continue to progress.

As the food crisis deepened and pay became erratic, concerns of the officers and enlisted men came to the fore. Many of them criticized the states for failing to honor the "Contract" between the government and themselves, i.e., in return for defending their country and enduring hardship, soldiers expected to have adequate provisions. Issues of rank, promotion and seniority amongst the officers further fostered unrest in camp. No clear system of promotion existed, therefore, disputes concerning appointments rankled the officer corps. Since officers provided most of their own necessities out of their own pockets and gave up civilian businesses and livelihoods for the cause, rank was especially important as a badge of distinction. General George Weedon of Virginia

James Mitchell Varnum (1748-89). Painting by Charles Willson Peale.

Lachlan McIntosh (1725-1806). Painting by Charles Willson Peale (1783-93).

attested that "a soldier's rank and reputation is all that's dear to him." Washington, for his part, was keenly interested in retaining quality officers. He had been pressing Congress for some time to enact a pension system as a means of attracting and keeping the best candidates. Although plagued by all of these divisive problems, no organized or collective dispute erupted—a sure testimony to the dedication of the American troops.

Coupled with problems of rank and regional differences among the troops, the need for a reorganization of regimental structure and uniform training also figured on Washington's list of necessary reforms. From the beginning of the war, he had been concerned about the importance of discipline and drill based on his French and Indian war experiences. He also recognized the need to adapt European military tactics to the American situation and terrain. Battle experience had shown the army needed help in coordination and close order drill. The army had been evolving into a professional force in the preceding two years based on changes initiated by Washington and enacted by Congress. Washington and his staff felt that it was time to take the next steps in their plans for further improving the army.

Gouverneur Morris (1752-1816). Edward Dalton Marchant copy after Sully (c. 1874). Morris, member of Congress from New York, arrived in camp in January 1778. He quickly became a strong advocate for the army.

From the beginning of January until the committee's arrival in camp on the 24th, Washington was intent on taking the offensive, aimed at Congress, about these problems. He was bent on ensuring permanence for the American Army.

The first meeting of the Committee on Conference and Washington's staff took place on January 28, 1778. Members of the committee were Francis Dana of Massachusetts, Nathaniel Folsom of New Hampshire, John Harvie of Virginia, Gouverneur Morris of New York, and John Reed of Pennsylvania. Together they comprised almost a quarter of the active members of Congress and represented a range of geographic locations and opinions. They brought with them, from their parent body, a broad mandate to work with Washington to initiate reforms throughout the military establishment. Simply by having Congress come to camp, Washington had won the first in a series of victories which were to secure the future of the American Army.

At the second meeting of the committee and headquarters staff, Washington presented his recommendations in a 38 page report entitled, "A Representation to the Committee of Congress." In it, he described the state of the Army and listed a series of reforms.

Officers

Officers, unlike enlisted men, provided most of their necessities out of their own pockets following European custom. They often suffered severe financial hardship as a result of this and the fact that they abandoned their civilian sources of income. Many complaints arose during the encampment about inflation and the exaggerated cost of keeping themselves properly outfitted and supplied.

The following are some of the objects that were typical of the property of an officer. Some items, such as epaulets, sashes, or gorgets, indicated rank; others, such as small swords, were badges of rank and served the practical purpose of self defense. Just like the enlisted men, they brought their personal belongings with them in an attempt to make military life as close to home as possible.

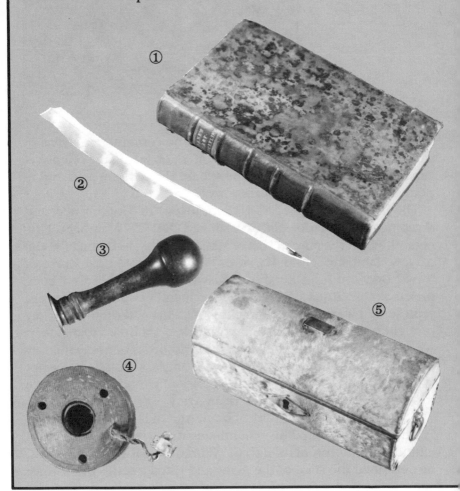

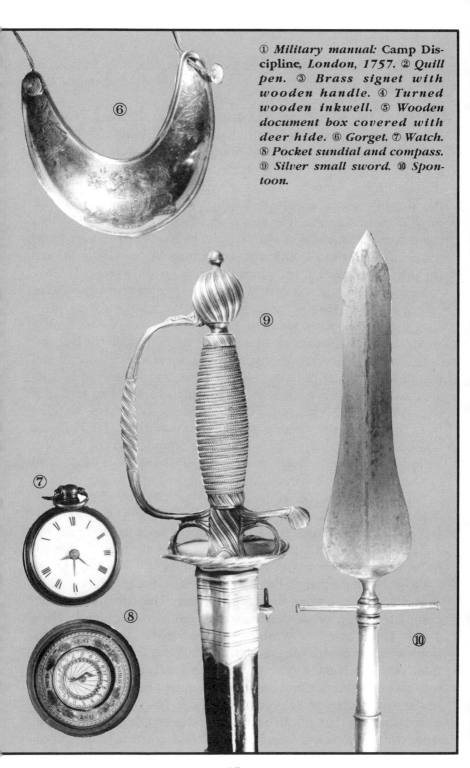

① *Military manual:* Camp Discipline, *London, 1757.* ② *Quill pen.* ③ *Brass signet with wooden handle.* ④ *Turned wooden inkwell.* ⑤ *Wooden document box covered with deer hide.* ⑥ *Gorget.* ⑦ *Watch.* ⑧ *Pocket sundial and compass.* ⑨ *Silver small sword.* ⑩ *Spontoon.*

In effect, he handed the committee their agenda, thereby placing himself in a position to control the topics of discussion and influence the solutions devised.

First on the agenda was the issue of quieting the disgruntled officer corps by setting up a "half pay and pensionary establishment." Washington felt strongly that this was a means of attracting and keeping sorely needed men of quality. Congress, on the other hand, worried about the expense of such a measure and the idea of creating a "standing army" by keeping soldiers on the payroll long after the war was over. Washington reported that there were frequent resignations due to hardships endured and financial insecurity. Adoption of such a measure could help to stem the tide of resignation and place the army on surer ground.

Next on the list of reforms, Washington proposed a new system of organization for the army as a whole. Among the reforms suggested were a reorganization and expansion of the cavalry service; the establishment of an office of the Inspector General with Brigade Assistants to institute a uniform system of drill and maneuvers; and, as per Congress' request, a reduction and standardization in military units. Washington also suggested that staff department posts, that required commissioned officers, be filled from the line. Those officers would then base their claim to rank and promotion on their place and performance in the line. He believed this would quiet complaints amongst the officers and further regularize the promotion system.

Finally, Washington addressed the problem of the support departments. He detailed their deficiencies, their organizational faults and repeated their fundamental importance to sustaining the army in the field. It was in this area that some of the most significant improvements were made during the winter.

Congress immediately began to address the issue of the almost complete breakdown of the supply system. They first requested a complete listing of all department personnel, their rank, their duties, and salaries. As Washington described it, the various support departments had engaged in an "extravagant rage of deputation." Not only had the system of assistants and deputies developed into an unproductive and sometimes corrupt bureaucracy, many of the top officials were completely inept. In addition, many key posts, such as that of Quartermaster General, had been vacant since the previous fall. Congress had failed to act on filling impor-

Nathanael Greene (1742-86). Painting by Charles Willson Peale (c. 1783). A native of Rhode Island, Greene accepted the post of Quartermaster General in February 1778.

tant appointments, and Committee members quickly determined that reform was necessary from the top down.

The true meaning of the system's inefficiency in camp was soon evident for the Congressmen to witness first hand. By the beginning of February, a food crisis befell the army. This crisis dwarfed any that the troops had experienced the previous fall. Committee members had to face the cold facts: the army consumed vast amounts of food and there was no mistake in the reports sent to Congress regarding their needs—indeed, the army had been subsisting from "hand to mouth" for some time. It finally became apparent to members of the government that the situation was critical and that measures to permanently resolve the problems were necessary to place the war effort on a sound footing. General Nathanael Greene described the transformation of the committee's attitude to Alexander McDougall in early February: "they came to camp with parliamentary prejudices, but stubborn facts and the condition of the army has wrought a wonderful reformation."

This dawning of reality on Congress not only spurred them into action on reforms, but also dramatically affected Washington's credibility. His incessant letters to Congress describing the plight of the army throughout the previous year had proven true. Better yet, due to him and his staff's preparations for the committee, tangible remedies were available and ready to be implemented. Over the next several months, members of the committee worked shoulder to shoulder with Washington and his staff to act on the proposals and move the Army on to some degree of permanence.

Congress undertook a complete reorganization of the Quartermaster Department which was responsible for acquiring and distributing those supplies that did not fall within the categories of food, clothing, arms and ammunition and for two vital services—the transportation of all supplies and moving and encamping the army. Without these two services, the army was helpless. It was imperative that deficiencies in this department be corrected; it was the cog on which the rest of the army turned.

The position of Quartermaster General had been vacant since Thomas Mifflin of Pennsylvania left in early fall 1777. The job of Quartermaster General was, for the most part, tedious and lacking in rewards. Field commanders with the skill and ability necessary to efficiently operate the department were wont to do so because of the nature of the task and the necessity of leaving direct command of the troops. George Washington recognized the department's needs and urged Congress to appoint a replacement for Mifflin.

During the month of February, the committee sought the best candidates available to fill the top posts in the support departments. They quickly appointed Jeremiah Wadsworth as new Commissonary General, responsible for the procurement of food, clothing, etc. They next set about the task of appointing a new Quartermaster General. Phillip Schuyler of New York was first considered as a replacement, however, his poor performance in the Northern Department of the Army, internal politics, and the weather soon sank his candidacy. During the first two weeks of February, the weather deteriorated and interrupted communications between camp and Congress at York, Pennsylvania. The committee rethought their choice of Schuyler and decided to interview another candidate, General Nathanael Greene of Rhode Island. Greene and the Committee conferred about the appointment in mid-February. Greene was then called upon by Washington to lead an emergency foraging expedition to remedy

Thomas Mifflin (1744-1800). Painting by Charles Willson Peale (1784).

Jeremiah Wadsworth (1743-1804). Painting attributed to James Sharples, Sr. (1795-1800). Wadsworth filled the post of Commissary General during the winter of 1778.

*———— a cet endroit l'arrivée forme une coude insensible qui porte son cour a l'est sudest ... la A

sont cet partis du retranchament se porte plus d'un...
la F

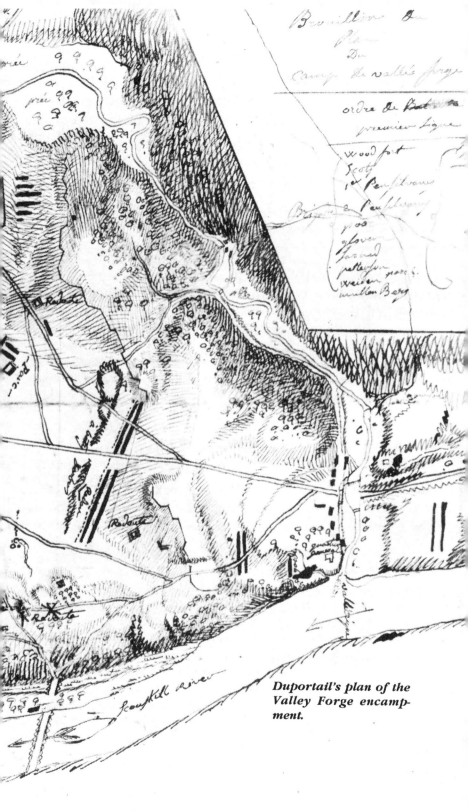

Duportail's plan of the Valley Forge encampment.

the food crisis being experienced by the army. Upon his return, Washington and the committee worked together to convince Greene to accept the post, as Greene was reluctant to leave his field command. By the end of February, Greene agreed to the appointment on the conditions that he name his two top assistants and maintain his field status. Greene and his assistants quickly began further reorganization of the department and spent the spring months busily preparing for the coming campaign. By installing this energetic, capable soldier at the helm, the committee had gone a long way toward putting the department on the proper course.

The issue of appointing an Inspector General and training the troops went hand in hand with the support department's preparation for the campaign season. Washington and his staff had long been planning reforms in the Army's discipline and drill. Debate hinged on further professionalization of the army or a return to a more militia based force. Further debate concerned the adoption of some European tactics and reform of American tactics. The Army already possessed sophisticated units due to the additions of engineers and cavalry. Relieved of the pressure of recruiting for the coming year, the time was right to act on the plans.

During the February food crisis, Baron Friedrich Von Steuben arrived in camp presenting his credentials as a veteran of European wars under Frederick the Great of Prussia. The Prussian Army, at that time, was considered one of the best professional armies in the world. Initially, Steuben was interviewed by Washington's aide, John Laurens, who felt that he was an excellent candidate for Inspector General.

Washington did not immediately determine Steuben's role with the army. Many foreign volunteers had previously claimed certain expertise which was not borne out in practice. In addition, placing a foreign officer in an important position, without "field-testing," could further antagonize the already disgruntled officer corps. The Commander-in Chief first sent Steuben on a tour of the camp to inspect its fortifications and make recommendations for their improvement and completion. Steuben established credibility with Washington based on his field inspection and demonstrated military knowledge. He further earned his respect by his willingness to serve as a volunteer.

Washington decided that Steuben was the proper individual to

Baron Von Steuben

Friedrich Wilhelm Von Steuben (1730-1794) arrived in the United States with a wealth of military experience gained in the Prussian army. He served under Frederick the Great in what was felt to be the most professional army in the world. Having suffered some reverses, Von Steuben was anxious to apply his knowledge and skills to the cause in America.

Von Steuben came to the camp at Valley Forge in February 1778. Within a short period, Washington assigned him the task of drafting a manual of arms for the troops and schooling them during the spring in preparation for the coming campaign. *Regulations for the Order and Discipline of the Troops of the United States* was formally published in 1779 and remained the basic manual for the American Army for the next 25 years. Von Steuben simplified and sharpened commands while borrowing elements of the English, French, and German systems to craft a new drill for the troops. He changed the basic formation from three ranks to two, as well, to enhance maneuverability. Overall, Von Steuben performed admirably and brought the Continental Army to a close approximation of its professional opponent.

Von Steuben.
Painting by Charles Willson Peale.

Enlisted Men

Men of the Continental Army came from all walks of life and ranged in age from those in their teens to their sixties. In essence, the army reflected the society of the new nation. Some enlisted because of their commitment to the cause; others sought the opportunities offered, such as cash or land bounties; and just as in other wars, many joined because they did not have better alternatives. Life in the military provided "regular" pay, food, and possibly a chance for adventure. Those who served during the Revolution often went on to serve their country after the war as local officials, or, later, as members of the new Federal Government. Experience gained by officers and enlisted men during the Revolution definitely aided in shaping the new nation.

The enlisted man carried his personal necessities on his back. Pictured here are typical objects found in almost any soldier's haversack. Beside's his own belongings, he carried his own weapon, the musket.

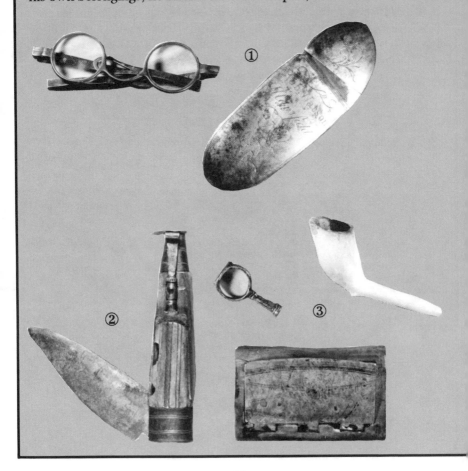

① *Eyeglasses and case.* ② *Pocket knife.* ③ *Brass pipe tamper, clay pipe, and tobacco or snuff box.* ④ *Horn cup.* ⑤ *Bone-handled knife and fork.* ⑥ *Pewter plate.* ⑦ *Large and small size pewter buttons.* ⑧ *Wooden and iron swigler.*

37

supervise the reform of the Army's discipline. Washington chose to introduce the system by first training a "model" unit and then moving on to the entire army. The unit consisted of Washington's own guard from Virginia plus an additional hundred men from the other state lines. To institute the new field drill throughout the army, a system of assistants and brigade inspectors was established.

By the end of March, drilling began. Regiments worked on their own parade grounds both in the morning and late afternoon. Later, exercises moved to the large central parade ground, called the Grand Parade. Emphasis was placed on the use of the bayonet and the institution of a uniform drill, both of which were essential to improved field performance; tactics and weapons determined the need for precise movements on the field. Washington supported the training exercises by placing increased emphasis on overall discipline within the army. These efforts combined with the experience of campaign seasoned soldiers and officers produced results within a few weeks. In a letter to his father, written at the beginning of April, John Laurens reported that Steuben was "making a sensible progress with our soldiers."

Having attacked two major obstacles to place the army on strong ground, Washington pushed the committee and Congress to pass his recommended reforms concerning regimental organization and a pension plan for officers. Congress deliberated over these matters well into the spring. It was not until late May that a new battalion structure and a reduced pension plan was agreed upon— too late for Washington to implement because the campaign of 1778 was about to open.

By the spring, Washington had achieved a number of important reforms. Why did these changes, long planned by the commander, finally occur at Valley Forge? As mentioned, they had the "leisure of a fixed camp" and were free of pressure to recruit for the coming year. The British, encamped in Philadelphia, did not actively pursue a campaign because they, too, had to recuperate after a hard campaign. The British also awaited the appointment of a new commander since Howe had asked to be relieved of his command. Overall, the problems of indecision coupled with the effects of campaigning held the enemy in check while the Americans worked toward their fighting trim.

The enemy's lack of action was not the only factor which affected the American's situation at camp. Washington capitalized on his political advantage and captured the attention of Congress through his dismal predictions about the possible fate of the army, and consequently, the future of America's hopes for independence. After arriving at camp, members of the committee witnessed, first hand, the food crisis and the marginal state of the army; a fundamental shift in attitude resulted. Washington and the staff at headquarters had also prepared a comprehensive plan for correcting most of the problems facing the American war machine. These plans and the force of Washington's personality affected the willingness of the committee to join in the effort to right this situation. Thus, the necessary foundation of cooperation was laid between the government and its military, and a major political victory was won.

Finally, the catalyst of a capable volunteer added to seasoned troops produced a fundamentally improved fighting force. Von Steuben contributed the right skills at the right time. He revised the manual of arms, directly supervised and trained soldiers and officers, and offered sound military advice to the staff at headquarters. Hard work throughout the spring forged the long sought result: a seasoned, effective, professional army.

Continental troops wore a variety of uniforms depending on rank and specialty.

A Day in the Life of the Military City

While Washington, his staff, and members of Congress took action on the issues facing the army as a whole, the daily life of the military city on the hills and fields of Valley Forge took shape. It may seem odd that two armies resided within a day's march of one another for nearly six months, but, in the 18th century, due to the lack of communication and the nature of transportation, it was customary for armies to cease fighting during the winter months. All 18th century armies suffered shortages which curtailed operations as men and equipment wore out from months of continuous battle. Additionally, during the encampment at Valley Forge, the British weighed their alternatives and remained in Philadelphia as they awaited directions from the mother country. In the meantime, the Americans constructed their log city to the west and prepared for an upcoming campaign.

The commonly held notion of a beaten and bedraggled Continental Army limping into Valley Forge is simply not borne out by the tremendous task undertaken of constructing the encampment and surviving in the face of severe material shortage. Only industrious, resourceful, and skilled men could have weathered such circumstances and managed to build a semi-permanent post.

The American soldier, having been recruited directly from civilian life, carried with him a variety of non-military skills which helped the army in its self-sufficiency. Shoemakers, tailors, coopers, farriers, and carpenters found employment during the encampment in helping meet the shortages facing the army and in preparing for the next campaign. The versatility of the Continental Army allowed it to survive despite the hardships it confronted.

In contrast, the British army was supplied with men possessing such skills, but they were in the minority. The primary task of the British officers and enlisted men was to perform in battle. Fighting thousands of miles from home, fundamentally they had only a single purpose—as a professional fighting unit.

From the outset, the encampment hummed with activity. Huts and fortifications appeared on the landscape, drillmasters shouted their orders, teamsters arrived bearing loads of equipment and supplies, express riders roared in, and forage parties marched out into the surrounding countryside. Keeping the army supplied, sheltered, protected, trained, and healthy, required constant activity.

On January 3, 1778, General Nathanael Greene wrote to his brother, Jacob, and said "...we are all going into log huts—a sweet life after a most fatiguing campaign." Within days of their arrival in December the men began building huts, and between December 21 and January 20 hut construction took precedence over most other activities in the encampment. Hundreds of huts were erected over a six to eight week period which conformed to Washington's own specific plan for their construction. Soldiers were broken up into twelve man squads, with each squad instructed to build its own hut measuring 16 feet in length, 14 feet in width, and 6 1/2 feet in height. They were constructed of logs chinked with clay and at the rear of each building was a fireplace also sealed with clay. The doors consisted of boards or split oak slabs; roofing material ranged from boards to saplings to earth supported by splints; and Quartermasters supplied straw for bedding. Construction was slowed by the lack of tools and draught animals to haul logs, but by the beginning of February Washington reported that most men were in huts.

Although Washington issued orders which detailed the construction of the huts, many variations on the model appeared in the camp. Since proper tools and materials were scarce, squads improvised roofs and other elements of their huts. Evidence found in period documents and archaeological investigations show that some huts were dug into the earth with their floors several feet below ground level and others were built with fireplaces in their corners. The diversity that appeared in the style of the huts may also be attributed to regional variation in building techniques; soldiers from North Carolina may have built their huts differently than those built by soldiers from another part of the country.

While the majority of the army lived in huts, some of the higher ranking officers made arrangements to stay in houses within the camp area. Some shared homes with families, and others rented structures for their homes. It was customary for general officers to seek housing to accommodate their staff and other aides. At Valley Forge, most found quarters on the southern edge of the camp where several farm houses were clustered. The Commander-in-Chief quickly discovered that the enormity of his workload

Reconstructed huts dot the landscape of the hills of Valley Forge. During the encampment, more than 1,000 huts were built within weeks of the army's arrival.

Washington's Headquarters, c. 1770. Washington rented the house for use as general military headquarters in December 1777.

demanded the necessity of a large structure to serve as his head-quarters. Within a week after his arrival at Valley Forge, the Isaac Potts house, located near the confluence of the Valley Creek and the Schuylkill River, filled this purpose. Washington rented the house from its occupant, Mrs. Deborah Hewes, thereby obeying his orders not to take advantage of civilians. He and his so-called "military family" of nine aides moved into the five room house which served as an office and home for his wife, staff, and the constant parade of visitors that he entertained.

Headquarters vibrated with activity throughout the encampment. Military orders for the entire army spread both north and south emanated from the house. Express riders, petitioners, visiting dignitaries, and all types of army officials continually passed through its doors. Within the house, Washington held councils with officers and politicians, wrote an average of 15 important letters per day, issued detailed daily General Orders, met with concerned citizens, and decided matters of military discipline. Almost every event that concerned the army originated from this location.

The layout of the camp was determined by military engineers. Regiments were aligned according to their order of march for battle and most huts housing soldiers were built in rows facing each other on company streets, with enlisted men's in front and officers' huts in a row behind them. Additional structures such as hospitals and slaughter pens also appeared within each brigade. Two main lines of defense traversed the camp area; an outer line that faced southeast toward Philadelphia along a high ridge, and an inner line that crossed the hills and stretched from Baptist Road to the edge of the Schuylkill River, which served as the northern boundary of the camp. (See map.)

The military engineers who designed the camp capitalized on the natural defenses of the area by laying out the camp with defensive lines and a planned system of fortifications. The arrangement of the huts and the fortifications was interdependent, and although no British attack ever materialized, the threat of an attack kept pressure on the army to fortify its position. Washington took this threat with much seriousness and urged the completion of the defensive works. Fatigue parties worked on construction of

Louis LeBeque DuPortail (1743-1802). Painting by Charles Willson Peale (1781-82). DuPortail, as chief military engineer, planned the layout of the defenses of the camp at Valley Forge.

Earthworks such as this redoubt on the inner line of defense played an important part in camp fortifications.

earthworks from the beginning of February and continued on into the spring. Progress was slow due to the harshness of the weather, but as the campaign season drew nearer and hints of British activity reached the camp, efforts were increased to complete the works.

As planned, studies indicate that a series of entrenchments, redoubts, and other obstacles supported the main lines of defense. Documents from the period indicate that there was debate over the location of some of the earthworks and that progress ebbed and flowed. Maps and other documentary evidence suggest that five major earthworks strengthened the defenses: two redoubts on roughly either end of the lines of defense, and a large "star" redoubt that overlooked the Schuylkill River at the northern end of the camp. These works, combined with the natural defensive features of the Valley Forge area, apparently presented a formidable obstacle to the enemy. Sir William Howe reported that the position was strong and did not favor an attack.

In addition to the fortifications, Washington dictated that a bridge across the Schuylkill River was needed to continue operations to the east, as well as to serve as a possible escape route. Construction began on the bridge on December 26, 1777, under

*Artillery park, centrally located in the center of the camp, served
as headquarters for artillery troops.*

the supervision of General John Sullivan. "Sullivan's Bridge," as it
was known during the period and afterward, required the efforts
of many skilled carpenters and axmen. They labored continuously
and completed the structure by the end of March 1778.

These numerous and varied construction projects accounted for
much of the activity of the camp, however, officers and soldiers
also used their skills to replace and repair equipment. Soldiers
involved in repairing weapons, artillery, saddlery, and building
barrels were known as artificers. Tailors and cordwainers
(shoemakers) plied their trades and helped to ease the clothing
needs of the enlisted men. Tanners worked hides that were left-
over from beef cattle and produced much needed leather for
straps, scabbards, and belts. And some soldiers found employment
in the laboratory making cartridges and musketballs. Obviously,
idleness was not a problem in the camp.

Added to the material needs of the army were the requirements
of those felled by sickness. Each brigade had a field hospital for
those not seriously ill and those recuperating from smallpox in-
oculation, which was carried out on a large scale basis late in the
winter by the Hospital Department. Surgeons and surgeon's mates

Henry Knox (1750-1806). Painting by Charles Willson Peale (c. 1783). Knox, a bookseller from Boston, assumed command of the Continental Army's Artillery early on in the war.

tended to the sick with the aide of women camp followers and soldiers' wives. Those who were more seriously ill were taken out of the camp to structures which were pressed into service as hospitals. The army also had established general hospitals in the area in locations such as Yellow Springs and Reading, which served those who were very ill and needed better care than could be provided in camp. The largest cause of death in the camp resulted from sickness and disease, as opposed to cold and starvation.

Washington continually stressed cleanliness and the necessity of privies in the brigade encampments. Orders dealt with removing disease-provoking refuse on a regular basis, as well as covering "necessaries" as needed. The urgency of refuse removal was strong because of the fact that animals were slaughtered within the brigade and thus posed a high risk for disease and other health hazards. This unclean environment, combined with the effects of other hardships, wreaked havoc on the army's health.

Fortunately, however, not all was unrelieved hardship during the encampment. Washington realized the benefits of establishing regular markets at several locations near the camp where soldiers could obtain fresh food and local farmers could trade with the

Camp Amusements

Not all was drill, patrol and fatigue duty at Valley Forge. Soldiers, often far from home, brought with them objects that helped to make life in camp bearable and, in some cases, enjoyable. Small items were easily carried in haversacks to be taken out in idle or lonely moments. Cards, marbles and hand-made diversions such as buzzers aided in passing time. Musical instruments such as a Jews Harp or tin whistle added much needed melodies to the daily drudgery of building and maintaining a fortified log city.

As in any army, gambling and its related problems occurred in camp. General Washington, always mindful of the importance of order and discipline, drafted numerous orders directed at stopping "gaming" throughout the Valley Forge encampment.

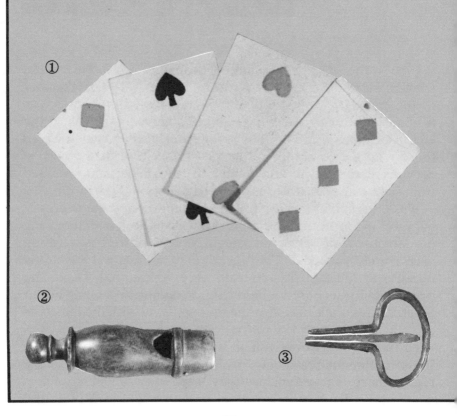

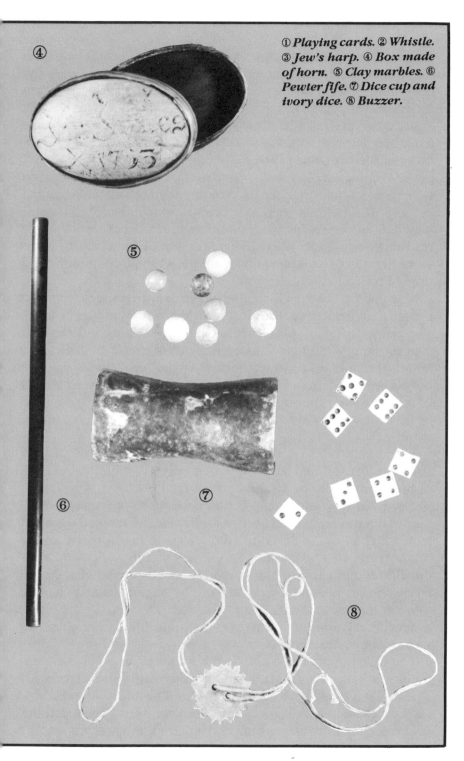

① *Playing cards.* ② *Whistle.* ③ *Jew's harp.* ④ *Box made of horn.* ⑤ *Clay marbles.* ⑥ *Pewter fife.* ⑦ *Dice cup and ivory dice.* ⑧ *Buzzer.*

④ ⑤ ⑥ ⑦ ⑧

could obtain fresh food and local farmers could trade with the Americans rather than the British. Markets were opened by the beginning of February and continued into the spring. Civilian sutlers also appeared in camp to provide supplements to the daily liquor ration of the soldiers, usually at a high price. Gaming became a popular activity in the camp as well, and officers had to enforce orders against it when problems occurred. "Women of the Army," as the Commander-in-Chief termed them, could only stay in camp when legitimately attached to a soldier or an officer and engaged in support functions such as a laundress or nurse. Washington watched all diversions closely and issued orders to regulate or restrict them as necessary. Discipline was of the utmost importance in order to maintain good relations with the community and uphold respect within the ranks.

Washington believed in treating civilians with respect and made certain that members of the army remained within proper bounds. The army depended on civilians for both political and material support, and Washington unceasingly directed through General Orders that soldiers conduct themselves properly and not venture out of the boundaries of the camp and their duties. Some instances of thievery and other infractions did occur, however, they were dealt with quickly through courts-martial and corporal punishment.

Throughout 1777 and 1778, civilians living in southeastern Pennsylvania suffered hardships as a direct result of the presence of both armies. Property and crops were destroyed, wagons impressed, fathers and sons recruited, supplies commandeered, homes overtaken to billet troops, and trade interrupted. General Jedidiah Huntington described the effects to his father by saying "...an Army, even a friendly one, if any can be called so, are a dreadful Scourge to any People—you cannot conceive what Devastation and Distress mark their Steps." The consequences of having two armies descend on a small area were undoubtedly great and as a result, relations between the civilian and military communities were, at best, strained.

The military city arose amidst the farming and industrial community of Valley Forge. The army created, within several months, a post that teemed with activity. Huts and fortifications went up, markets came into existence, more soldiers were recruited, training began, equipment was built and repaired, and preparations for the coming campaign proceeded apace. Rather than succumbing to the shortages, hardships, and problems, the Continental Army managed to thrive and rebuild; the forge of experience served them well.

Marquis de Lafayette (1754-1834). Painting by Charles Willson Peale (1781), replica.

Legal Tender

During the American Revolution, the definition of legal tender, other than hard coin, was difficult to determine. The continental Congress and states both issued notes. Unable to secure loans or mint necessary coins, paper currency was printed to meet the needs of daily business and trade. Quickly, paper money lost value because of the chaos brought on by war and counterfeiting. Inflation was also rampant by the late 1770s making the phrase "not worth a continental," part of everyone's vocabulary. This situation, as well as political problems, organizational deficiencies and the tremendous material needs of the army, contributed to the difficulties faced during the encampment.

Every denomination of Continental Currency had its own unique emblem and motto on the front. The backs were decorated with nature prints of leaves. All of this currency was printed in Philadelphia, home of the Continental Congress for most of the war, except the Feb. 26, 1777 (Baltimore) and the April 11, 1778 (York, PA or "Yorktown") issues.

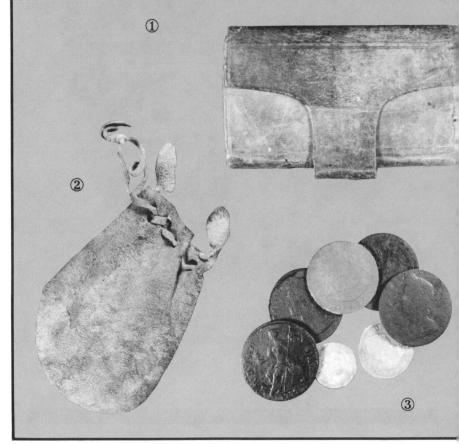

① *Leather wallet.* ② *Buckskin bag.* ③ *English copper and Spanish silver coins. Continental Currency:* ④ *$7, issue of Feb. 26, 1777.* ⑤ *$30, May 20, 1777.* ⑥ *$20, April 11, 1778.* ⑦ *$6, April 11, 1778 (back).*

④

⑤

⑦

⑥

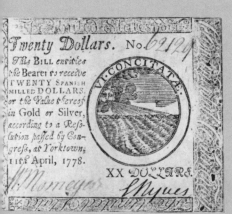

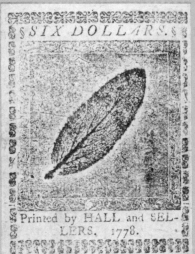

As the Campaign Season Approaches

As spring marched on, efforts doubled toward ensuring readiness for the coming campaign. Reforms in support departments were successful as food and other supplies poured into the camp, and during the first few weeks of April, daily drilling under the new system produced marked improvement in the skills of the soldiers. Washington's repeated requests for more men eventually resulted in troops arriving to reinforce those already in camp. Committee members continued to urge Congress to act on the remaining reforms yet to be passed, and the hint of a possible British attack fueled work on completing the fortifications. The army continually prepared to meet the challenge of the enemy.

As Quartermaster General, Nathanael Greene labored feverishly to see that supplies got to camp and that preparations for the army's imminent move were underway. His most important task was to make sure of the army's mobility—both for the men and their materials. The business was daunting at times, as reported in Greene's remarks to Congressman Gouverneur Morris in late spring: "I have drawn on the Treasury already for upwards of four millions of dollars, and it seems to be but a breakfast for the department, and hardly that." In May, Washington ordered that supply magazines by set up along the way into New Jersey because they could insure the army's lifeline and speed up its pursuit of the British once their objective was made clear. It was Greene's job to oversee this task, and he completed it as ordered.

Throughout the spring, the British waited for direction from the home office. Howe had submitted his resignation and awaited the King's acceptance, as well as the naming of his successor. The British Government was in the midst of rethinking the war effort since no immediate prospects for conclusion seemed near, but events soon conspired which pushed them into action.

An alliance between France and America had been a possibility for some time, and although the French aided the war effort with both supplies and military experts from early on in the war, a formal declaration of support and alliance had yet to be signed. Negotiations proceeded throughout 1777 and America's victory over Saratoga in October 1777, provided a catalyst for the agreement. Terms were agreed upon in February 1778. Washington received news of the alliance on May 1, and official notification from Congress followed shortly thereafter. The alliance was announced to the troops in General Orders on May 5 and the following day was set aside for a grand celebration.

This celebration provided the perfect opportunity to demonstrate the army's accomplishments under the new system. Washington ordered all troops to march, in order of brigade, to the Grand Parade ground. Once assembled, they formed two lines and presented a *feu de joie*, or running musket fire. Added to this display were shouts of the army "huzza" and salutes to the King of France, the "friendly European powers and the American states." It was a great day of rejoicing as reported by contemporary observers, such as Charles Willson Peale, who wrote:

> May 6 Went to Camp to see the Rejoicing for the Good News from France—The Troops was paraded and marched to hear a Short discourse adapted to the Occation—afterwards they grounded their Arms, and that [being] a signal Cannon was fired and each division Marched to the Ground alloted for them which in the Whole formed two lines—at another Cannon being fired as a signal, thirteen Cannon was discharged, and then a Runing fire begining at the Right & going to the left—of the front Line & from the left to the right of the 2d line and 3 huzzas for the King of France, the 13 Cannon fired & and Runing fire 4 huzzas for the States of America—after which each Brigade marched to their quarters, to be Regaled—the Officers of each Brigade then Walked thirteen abrest with musick to the Arnolds where a Cold Colation was provided for them. I had forgot to mention that his Excellency went with his Retinue along the Lines before the firing began, each Redgement Saluting him as he passed them—And the [parade] was ended with much mirth & good humour. I cannot say that I ever see more pleasure in as great a Number of faces at any one time—Ld Stirling Commanded on the Right of the front Line The Marquis de la Fiate on the left & and the Baron de Cald [Kalb] the 2d line—Baron Stubin [Steuben] superintended—

France's formal declaration for the United States prompted the British high command to make decisions about pursuing the war effort. In order to avoid war with France, the British had to scale back their objectives in North America, and they also had to consider their interests in Canada and the Caribbean. They chose to focus on these areas and fundamentally altered the course of the war. Sir Henry Clinton assumed command and was told to engage the Americans in a general and decisive action. Once that was concluded, Clinton was to proceed to New York and embark on a sea campaign to harass and interrupt trade along the New England coastline. In the meantime, a peace commission made its way to the United States to try to negotiate a settlement short of recognizing the country's independence. These negotiations continued into June.

As these maneuvers went on behind the scenes, Washington called a Council of War on May 8 to poll his officers on their opinions on a course of action. The alternatives he put before them were to attempt to take Philadelphia; to move toward New York, which seemed a likely British objective; or to stay at camp and wait to see what action the British might take. He also told them that the British had about 10,000 troops in Philadelphia, 4,000 in New York, and 2,000 in Rhode Island; the Americans anticipated having 20,000 troops. The officers decided that the army should remain in camp in order to use the time for further training and provisioning until the enemy moved, and so they waited.

Drilling the troops at Valley Forge.

Charles Willson Peale

Artist, inventor, naturalist and Revolutionary War soldier, Charles Willson Peale (1741-1827) captured the faces of independence. He was the first to paint General Washington and created the image of the Commander-in-Chief that most of his contemporaries recognize. For the museum he began in the 1780s, Peale systematically recorded the faces of the leaders of the Revolution for his "Gallery of Illustrious Personages." He felt that by studying the likenesses of these accomplished individuals, visitors to his museum gained inspiration to guide their own lives.

Peale, a Philadelphian, visited the camp at Valley Forge frequently. He busied himself making oil portraits and miniatures of many of the officers and their visiting wives. He also recorded camp scenes in his diary. His description of the May 6th celebration gives us one of the most vivid accounts of the activities staged on the Grand Parade.

Charles Willson Peale, self-portrait (c. 1778).

Practical Proof

From May 15 on, the Americans knew the British were planning to abandon the city. They prepared to follow, suspending exercises after May 20. The British suffered delays because of the complexity of moving a large force and waiting to hear the outcome of the peace negotiations. Some skirmishing took place as both sides feinted real action.

As the Americans scrambled to assemble needed supplies, arms and accoutrements, campaign preparations reached fever pitch. As part of the transition to field status, the army moved from huts into tents on June 9 and 10. The arrival of additional troops swelled the ranks and made shelter scarce. After nearly six months, the camp area was filthy and unhealthy as well, and therefore, Washington ordered work parties to clean it up.

He put support departments on alert and ordered troops into New Jersey to raise the militia and stop the anticipated advance of the enemy toward New York. Based on intelligence concerning British movements and the status of peace negotiations, the army held its tenuous position hovering at the ready. The tension created by preparing for war while patiently waiting eventually wore on the army. John Laurens described it as "...a most tiresome time of inactivity and suspense."

In mid-June, Congress debated the British offer of peace terms. The American position maintained that the country's independence must be recognized or no settlement could be reached. The British negotiators had permission to grant all concessions except that one. Hence, the peace terms were rejected on June 17, 1778, and the wheels of both military machines went into motion.

News of the British evacuation of the city on June 18 travelled quickly. Washington dispatched two brigades instructed to follow closely on the heels of the enemy with the rest of the army ready to do the same the following day. General Benedict Arnold received the order to take a small occupying force into the city on June 19. The chase was on.

The British made slow progress across New Jersey giving the Americans time to consider their next move. On June 24, Washington called a Council of War to discuss alternatives. He reported that both sides possessed about 10,000 regulars and an attack could be staged. The general officers debated the feasibility of an action and voted against it. Washington, however, disagreed and ordered that an attack be made if "fair opportunity offered."

The opportunity came on June 27, 1778, when Washington determined to attack the following day near the Monmouth County Courthouse. General Charles Lee commanded the advance troops. Lee, not having faith in the ability of the Continentals to meet the British in an open contest, failed to execute his orders. Washington, infuriated, followed up along with General Greene's regiments. The Americans showed their newly acquired skills by forming with precision and speed. The troops continued to advance and drove the professionals back. At the end of the day, they held the field and the British slipped away under cover of night. The Continental Army then had practical proof of improvements made during the preceeding months.

The significance of the events at Valley Forge lies in the strides taken toward building a professional army—one for the duration of the war. The army that arrived in December 1777, possessed raw strength, skill, and determination. These characteristics combined with organizational reform, a uniform system of drill, training, talented and dedicated officers, and an effective, politically adept commander resulted in great and capital changes for the American military. The winter encampment, indeed, was one of several turning points during the American Revolution; one which proved the mettle of the Continental Army and, eventually, secured independence.

Muskets

The musket was the most important firearm of the American Revolution. Regular infantry, on both sides, carried this weapon. The musket was a single-shot smoothbore muzzleloader; it was 4 to 5 feet in length, had a caliber of .69 to .80 and was fired by a flintlock mechanism. To load a musket, soldiers used a paper cartridge loaded with powder and a round lead ball. The musket could be loaded and fired rapidly; a well trained solder was expected to load and fire four times per minute. In that era, it was considered a fine weapon.

Muskets were accurate up to a range of about 50 yards. This fact determined tactics used when in battle. Infantry soldiers formed in two lines, shoulder-to-shoulder, with a line of file-closers in the rear to take the place of those who fell. Soldiers loaded and fired on command. The theory was to lay down a field of fire rather than to aim and shoot. After a series of volleys, a bayonet charge was mounted and a battle ended in hand-to-hand combat. Highly trained soldiers who moved precisely and quickly on command usually held the field. At Valley Forge, Von Steuben worked diligently on schooling the troops in this important close order drill system.

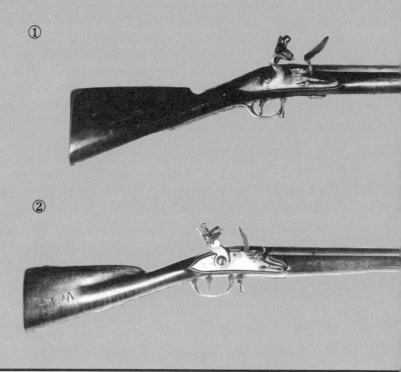

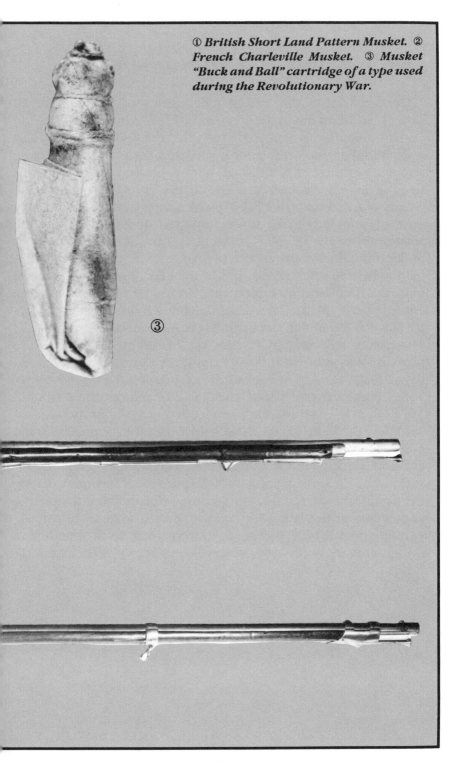

① *British Short Land Pattern Musket.* ② *French Charleville Musket.* ③ *Musket "Buck and Ball" cartridge of a type used during the Revolutionary War.*

③

The Making of a Monument

George Washington visited the remains of the Continental Army's encampment in the summer of 1787, during a break in the Constitutional Convention. He recorded the visit in his diary and remarked that the fortifications were in ruins and not much else remained of the camp; although he was pleased to see the fields once again under cultivation. Thus began visits to remember the events of the winter of 1777-78. From early in the 19th century onward, people felt that it was important to commemorate the accomplishments of the Continental Army that were achieved under difficult circumstances. As early as 1828, ceremonies were held in honor of the troops, and by the mid-19th century, several individuals had begun a campaign to preserve and memorialize the encampment. As the Centennial Celebration drew near, the Centennial and Memorial Association was formed for the purpose of purchasing and saving Washington's Headquarters. Once the property was safely in "public" hands, the movement progressed to set aside, forever, the grounds used during the winter camp. Valley Forge became a state park in 1893 and remained so until 1976 when the National Park Service acquired the property.

Today, the Valley Forge National Historical Park preserves the core of the 18th century encampment area and the story of the accomplishments of the Continental Army. Research and preservation activities are ongoing with the purpose of further revealing the significant themes that the resources tell us about the people and events of the late 18th century. Archaeologists, historians, exhibit specialists, curators, and interpreters work together to bring the story to life and preserve the vestiges of the camp for future generations.

Dogwoods at the New Jersey Monument, Valley Forge National Historical Park.

Suggested Readings

Alden, John Richard. *The American Revolution, 1775-1783*. New York: Harper Bros., 1954.

Billias, George A. *George Washington's Generals*. New York: Morrow, 1964.

Boatner, Mark May, III. *Encyclopedia of the American Revolution*. New York: David McKay Co., 1966.

Carp, E. Wayne. *To Starve the Army at Pleasure: Continental Army Administration and American Political Culture, 1775-1783*. Chapel Hill: University of North Carolina Press, 1984.

Cunliffe, Marcus. *George Washington: Man and Monument*. Boston: Little, Brown, and Co., 1957.

Kohn, Richard H. *Eagle and Sword: The Beginnings of the Military Establishment in America*. New York: The Free Press, 1975.

Jackson, John W. *Valley Forge: Pinnacle of Courage*. Gettysburg: Thomas Publications, 1992.

Mitchell, Joseph B. Discipline and Bayonets: *The Armies and Leaders in the War of the American Revolution*. New York: GP Putnam's Sons, 1967.

Neumann, George C. and Frank J. Kravic. *Collector's Illustrated Encyclopedia of the American Revolution*. Harrisburg: Stackpole Books, 1975.

Peterson, Harold L. *The Book of the Continental Soldier, Being a Compleat Account of the Uniforms, Weapons, and Equipment with which He Lived and Fought*. Harrisburg: Stackpole Co., 1968.

Royster, Charles W. *A Revolutionary People at War: The Continental Army and American Character, 1775-1783*. Chapel Hill: University of North Carolina Press, 1980.

Trussell, John B.B., Jr. *Birthplace of an Army: A Study of the Valley Forge Encampment*. Harrisburg: Pennsylvania Historical and Museum Commission, 1976.

Wright, Robert K. *The Continental Army*. Center of Military History, Washington, DC, 1983.